ON ROUTE TO
LEAMENEH

ON ROUTE TO LEAMENEH

FRANK GOLDEN

Raven Arts Press/Dublin

On Route to Leameneh
is first published in 1990 by
The Raven Arts Press
P. O. Box 1430
Finglas
Dublin 11
Ireland

ISBN 1 85 186 084 3

Raven Arts Press receive financial assistance from The Arts Council (An Chomhairle Ealaíon) Dublin, Ireland.

Grateful acknowledgements are made to the editors of the following papers and journals where some of these poems first appeared:
Poetry Ireland Review, Sunday Tribune (New Irish Writing) and *Poetry Australia*. A selection appeared in *Twelve Bar Blues (Raven Introductions 6).*

The author would like to express his thanks to Mary and Bernard Loughlin and all the staff at Annaghmakerrig for the generosity extended to him over the past number of years.

Cover detail from "The Edge" by Paddy Graham. Cover design by Rapid Productions. Illustrations by Paddy Graham. Design by Dermot Bolger & Aidian Murphy. Printed and bound in Ireland by Colour Books Ltd., Baldoyle.

£99914 / 821 Gol

£4·95

CONTENTS

Part I

Lorca...11
Some Bondage Is Nice...19
The Terror Of Disunities...22
A Story For Children..25
Shaman Fever 1B Fort Washington Avenue................27
Love Or Bedamned...30
He Begins to Moves Away..32
No Two Are The Same...33
For All That Has Gone Before..................................35

Part II

Beside Himself..39
Rose Garden Addendum..41
Colder Than Death..43
Terminal..44
Dead Sheep On The Hill...45
A Home For Itself...47
The Word According To God.....................................49
A Just And Holy Kill..50
It's Very Simple..52

Part III

Eliza Eliza...55
Sing Sing O My Most Chastened Heart......................57
Breviary For A Summer Night..................................58
The Men Of Clare Now Drink Their Porter
    On The Palisades...59
Buttock To Buttock..60
The Youngest Of My Most Mournful Lovers................61
Maura Rua..63

Both "Illustrated Corpses" and "Death by Hanging" which form part of the poem "Dead Sheep on the Hill" derive from the "In Dublin" film guide, from which they were cut out and pasted onto one of Paddy Graham's paintings.

Foreword

In 1988, after my return from New York, I worked in Temple Bar Gallery and became familiar with the work of Paddy Graham. Before leaving for Clare in August of that year I spent some time alone in his studio. I had an idea to work on a series of poems related to his paintings. The poems which resulted from this visual ingestion later became the meditastive centrepiece of "On Route To Leameneh". The painting loosed me from an old poetic articulation. They pressed me forward. However Paddy's influence goes far beyond his paintings, he is substantially present in every part of the book. In acknowledgement of this debt and in gratitude, I dedicate the book to him.

Frank Golden, 1990.

For Paddy Graham

PART I

y cuando quiere ser medusa el platano
ire a Santiago
Lorca

LORCA SINGS A CANTO ON LUDLOW RECALLING HIS EX NOW RESIDENT ON THE NORTHERN TIP OF THE BURREN

I'll hit out for Gleninsheen
Rather than heel it on First
Blow bills and blush kisses
To the revenant on Seventh
Carburet my lung packs
Fill my stomach at Katz
Watch the kosher be kosher
Fill their suburban princesses
With hot dogs, sauerkraut,
and jeweljellied cheesecake
While their seeded blood mothers
Get pressurized and hot
Settle their boobs like
Buttocks on the counter top
Chomp on flamefingered burgers
Slake their thirst with seltzer
Spread their bagels with creamcheese
Their pickles with mustard
Try to eat to the point
Where it solaces their hurt.
These women are big
These women are fur bound
Bulging at the seams
With lurid fat contours
Rippling jowls
And icecream temptations
On the tips of their tongues.
"Chocolate chip Buddy
An' hold the fudge sauce."

While their fingers clink glass beads
and baubles.
Gifts from their honies
Whom you'd think must be sweet
As only honies can be sweet
But they're not,
Not really, not anymore.

11

O their men never
Teasingly tumble them down
Onto sofas or waterbeds
They're just never around
To lovingly tender
The thrust of their lust
And say "Baby
I want to eat you
Where you're hot,
With soft hazelnut butter
And grade A Canadian Maple Syrup."
O they're just not silly anymore
Maybe they never were.

They do their business
With liquorice wallets
Slide down to the river
Looking for something more sacred
Than peppered beef,
Their eyes on Essex
Lips on barrels of brine
Hands with an action so sweet
They crank an old song
From a good girl.

O grant me the requisite
Gift for departure
I'll take my eyes from the sourdough
Rise with the sun
Coming up over Battery Park.
I've had it with this town.
Now that winter's hit
I can feel it on the street,
Stones turning white
Blood in the underground,
Folks on the Bowery
With squeegees and window wipes
Looking for a little Thunderbird
To heal their thirst.
Come January they'll be
Fleshless and sore

And the city shelter's no good,
"You just get beat up."
I can see them remember
The sun of their childhood,
Warm and Sugary
Melting over Indiana,
With cherries in the fruit field
Blueberries in the hog dell
And Mama smackin' her lips.

When Winter hits
I can feel it on the street,
Tyrone boys got their money
Tied up on B
With the goods to load
Your arms with gold.
They smoulder on corner stones
Tempt you on Bleeker
Making for soft holes and lust bowls
Down by Chicky's new place,
Climbing with street girls
To the top floor
For a view of East Houston sunshine
And Goldstein's Funeral Parlour,
Green velvet and satin
Where delicate boys groove
Like Necros on crack.
An' Dora she's junked out
Dora's the black girl.
She's high on cocaine
Stung me for money
"And love you're my honey
But life it ain't easy.
I wanna change see
I wanna change it all
See what comes next
But I lost my lenses
In the voodoo chicken hut
Under Williamsburg Bridge
An' Africa's really my home.
Where's your home Baby?

13

Where's your home?
O I've lost my lenses and
my senses,
I can only see what's burnin'
and runnin',
So go baby get me some speed
I'll be blissful ever after
With you Baby believe me."

O I want to go home
Be there for the Springtime
See vines on the hill
See stars in the water
See fields and red apple groves
Blue grass on the mountain.
I want to flee this town
All it breeds is lemon tears
Steel drum heat blisters
And cruel poems from the poets
who collect on Rivington
Under Wintry pineapple skies
Moaning lazy heartrending lullabies
With garbage sticking to their ribs
And poor Orion like a goatherd gone bad
Messing himself in the square.
An Israeli confabulationist
Trying not to let too much reality
In the peephole, he says;
"Green odium taints the sternest oraculars
Salivating sucktile solipsisms."
O Orion you're the only poet
I know in New York city,
You can feel the heat
You can smell the bad organs
Everyone's got one;
From Fifth Avenue gallstones
To Lexington Livers
And east Village poses
That strain the buttocks,
From mail order cancers
To Cartier viruses

All the best secrets
Remain in the blood.
"Do you really want what's goin' down?
Best stick with your own meat."
Me, I'm going down to see
My lady on Eleventh.
Lovers on Ludlow leave nothing to chance
They know their limitations
They just want to dance.
"Hold me Baby. Don't ever leave me.
All I got are my cat toys, kitties and creams.
No one will ever walk across
The crystal floor again.
So stay Baby. You've got to stay.
Fold my hands in yours
Lay them in the oven,
Let's make like we're bonding forever."

No way Jose.
Time will crab your voice
Until you're lined up
With the heartsinkers,
And maybe the best we had
Was bliss for you
But it gave me permanent indigestion.
Maybe if I'd been older
Or you'd let your skin go wild
In the sharpest morning.
I don't know Baby,
There's no sunshine here
To dry your pores.

Now when I cry on Ludlow
To the braying sound
Of poor Dominican women
Trying to haul the ghetto
Up from its knees,
I can smell my own loneliness.
I hear the best ideas crack
And my nails grow into jelly moulds.
I feel my whole body rot

15

Frank Golden

From the inside,
Turn out in the East River
On the Brooklyn side
Over by Domino's sugar plant,
The city's eyes
Floating on refuse fleets,
The lights of midtown
Like bright airpack bubbles
Protecting a fragile height,
Steadying truncated eagles
in the air,
While I move as a soluble goo
The crystal epidermal layers
stirred in the pot.

But it's more than loneliness
That makes me think of you.
I find I call your name
In secret places;
Under electric signs on Stuyvesant,
On Delancy when the lights go green,
Through flop house windows
on Fourteenth.
But the nearest living things
Are roaches and waterbugs
The sound of burlesque on B
Hard piano from Sophie's backroom
And Lurie's Lizards
With sax spilling in rain.
I hit on the same chicks
Step over acid stools
And messy two-storey suicides,
Walk through needle park
Over to Odessa where panhandlers
Watch the zentrail of urine
And drunks fevered and bloody
Melt tarmac with breath spits.
The worm in the bottom
Moves up through midtown,
Through Sushi bars
Under hot Indian canopies

Harsh Korean fruit stalls
And Polish Diners.
The city's feasting on sweat
And corralled lust.
"Let's be safe Baby
But don't touch me where it hurts.
O Sweet! Sweet!
This must be how lovers love."

Where are you now
My old lady from Eleventh?
Ludlow sings for you
Ludlow cries for you.
I sing for you.
I cry for you.
Atlantic fishes telegraph my need
I'll hop on a porpoise
Pit stop in Portland
Then it's North Clare
Or a watery grave.
I can smell those mussels
Piled high and steaming
In Nicky Mosse's bogbrown bowls
Laced with garlic and fennel.
O do you still think of me Baby?
Is the terror still there for you?
I could still bleed for you,
breed in you.
"Come back Paddy Reilly
Light a candle in my heart
Love me in the white water."

I'll hit out for Gleninsheen
Rather than heel it on First.
Don't want to winter here
The walls teeming with tears,
Women loaded up on Hagen Daz
And mint oriel cookies
Trying to pacify the blood.
I'll go back to you in North Clare
Eat mussels by the water's edge

And believe we could make it
To the far point past Muckinish
Out to the stranded Martello
black in November light,
A rigid symbol in the blue blue sea
For maudlin beauties
To stand and look back on it all.

SOME BONDAGE IS NICE

He dreams of a roué Queen
He'd seen on A and Sixth
Stiletto heels, a sequined bottom,
Boobs that juggled nightmares,
Eyes full of audacious rites
Nails like maraschino cherries,
A tongue of boiled port,
A body ready to flail itself
In a dance of spurs and postures,
Leather squeezing silicon
Implants and celuliteless thighs,
Feet stepping over cloudberry bottles,
Drunks clammy with excitement.
A young boy with a roman towel
Over his crotch
Lies at the broad end of the bar,
Cuffs of spiked felt tying his wrists.

The crowd mills around the bar-room counter
Lights low, a mush of faces in the tinted glass,
Urine, talc and beer weighing the air.
Spiked catfish men lever their crotches,
Telling the maiden Queen to feast.
"Do it Baby. Curl down."
She's burning now, heels like tap studs
Singing the risk of her gestures,
Eyes like steel buttons on a cocaine roll,
Head back singeing leather.
She loose now, loose as butter,
Loose as a good girl gone wild.
She'll take it all.
Standing over the boy
She secretes her fingers,
Kinks his hair,
Trounces him with the cat-tails and screams.
The crowd,
Bonded by defiance,
Yells,
"Rip it off.

Rip it off."
The towel stays on,
The only sacred thing in this room,
Suspending everything,
Waiting to be elevated,
In one immaculately crisp movement.
A free range huckster in feathers
Sinisters her ear.
"Be holy Baby," he whispers
As she kneels,
Takes the white knot in her teeth,
Jerks,
Frees his privates
And rocks back.

In maroon light
Alphabet men stare at the penis
Limp between the young boy's legs.
A decrepit Dean Martin lookalike
Grooves a grotesque insect dance
Around an addict waif,
Her arms spiraling like woodliced oak,
Hip bones sharp as wasp stings
Through black latex,
Head in the dance,
Feet scalding white tiles
While peacock bloods
Sip cool blue martinis
Spilling rumours of the Queen.
Spreading spittle on her thighs,
Singes of fire on her feet.
Tellin' her to grind down
And make it.
The crowd becomes despondent
Beginning to fantasize with itself.
She tries again, going down, head
Between his legs, letting her nails
Sink to the crescents in his flesh.
They want the thing engorged,
Pleasure made for them in the round.
Flustered she dribbles

The penis out of her mouth,
Stands back and flails,
The tails fleshing the air with screams.
Cries on the crest of pain,
The crest of love.
Love cries.
The bonds released.
Blood slavered from the counter
Like fresh sherbet.
Lights!
Lights down.

L 99914/821 gol

Frank Golden

THE TERROR OF DISUNITIES

From the four poster bed
The door to the ivory bathroom opened,
A hint of fern-green filigree, then nude.
Still shy she turns the room dark.
"If you see the flaws you'll love me less."
So she crept like a muskrat underneath
the covers
Whispering this ancient theory of deception
And by an inverse logic of harmony.
But harmony was the lightest pulse between us.
When I saw her I was afraid.
I see her now swim in the bed
Threatening to touch me.
If you touch me I will char.
If you kiss me my eyes will burn out.
If you lie on top of me the world will end.
All of the boiled food at my centre
Will rise into your french mouth.
You will diminish me utterly.
Is there any other way I can say it?
You will diminish me.
In darkness I see her crawl on top,
Sinking down on the body.
Love!
Love at this limit yields to disgust,
Your body a declaration of hope,
Your eyes demanding we reclaim the best
of ourselves
And love luminously, love like crackerjacks,
Brilliantly synthesized.
But your love lumps my back in pimples,
Makes the whole commotion soluble,
Legs dead, the laboured heart elsewhere,
A discipline of deception,
With the self deceived languorous
And still honied, still deceived.
There is no hope love.
Go. Pack your charm bracelets, cat relics
and couture.
Leave me.

For years we ran the gamut of heartbreak and
reconciliation,
Tragedies bolstering the stature of our bond,
A physical fixture leaning instinctively
To the right man, the right woman,
Which we were not, but we were bound
To the precious idea of the ideal bond,
Love with the least strategy,
An illogical love without envy.
Our final efforts were to make the thing
so bad,
The love thing so cracked and alien
That guilt could be shouldered,
And the structure gradually razed.
The reality behind this abnegation
Meant a pruning down of true stories,
Things as they were,
So that for a time we remained
The Good, the Loved, the Loveable,
The unfulfilled, the deceived,
While passion faltered, love receded.
The final dissolution was covert.
At daybreak I slipped out of New York,
Headed for Kennedy,
My heart like a billhook
Snagged in the breast,
Still deceived to the point
Where I believed I would return.
After all everything I owned was there,
Effigies, icons, fish slice.

When I regurgitate parts of the whole
I see it was a love without improper revelations.
Whatever harmony we contrived
Meant that we were unbelievably 'other'
in that harmony.
You said;
"I want to know only so much as I can survive with."
You said;
"I want us to be bonded by all that is good.
I don't crave the details of your past.

23

Frank Golden

I love you.
Don't leave me.
We can work past this.
After all isn't it in the nature of relationships
That they are difficult, problematical,
That the love bond is deepened and partly
measured
By the pain endured."

A STORY FOR CHILDREN

Love strikes in the marble cleft
An ancient greeness fruited behind.
Remembering vestibules of swift
Action, teeth chip for blood.

In red years toad swallowings
Made the vibrant difference.
We sat on glabrous leaves
And sang waterly among white colonnades.

When there were more aggrieved men
Than women to suffice,
I lamented my eyes through the window
And Romeo'd your tongue onto my nipples.

Men demented for love swung
Rural fists nubbling the plaster.
Between warbling screams people
Tumbled on the deal stairs.

Women fretted that domestic anger
Would unhinge the clear toned chandelier,
That solvent anger would flow the streets
And dogs bolt with the spirits of
unmastered girls.

Women stood in delux gardens
Choosing their life's mirror.
Men defining revenge exhaled
Glass in slivers to the stars.

In the green room leaves
Thickened on our skin,
Red berries brought trees of birds
And love disgorged in volumes from our
parts.

Had love been less custodial
Vital trees might have fruited twice,

25

But the diamond factor of your tongue
Split our starred reflection.

In the architecture of white dreams
I idolize our green coupling,
In the blue atmosphere of recorded love
Our gardened flesh decays.

SHAMAN FEVER 1B FORT WASHINGTON AVENUE

All that exists lives.
The lamp walks around.
The walls of the house
Have voices of their own
Even the chamber vessels
Have a separate land.
Borgoras

I've been alone for twenty days and twenty nights.
My lovers telephone and tell me they can see my shadow
spawning out over the roof of the building.
"What colour is it?" I ask.
Their concern is hysterical.
They tell me to eat outrageously, eat at all cost,
as though food would sensually retard my dedication
to see this event through to its end.
They ask whether they can come over, fix me some muffins
or pecan pie perhaps.
Home bake tack to deposit in the john.
Their understanding is that if I see my own shit I'll be
suddenly grounded.
"Haven't I told you" I reply, "that I only eat prepared
sections of raw buffalo packed with quartz crystals.
In this way I will be a centre of light when the light
shines.
Besides I feel too desperate to eat."
I lie naked on the green divan in an otherwise empty
livingroom, waiting for the Polar Bear to come
and chew me up.
I've seen him from the window stalk the shellaced
counters
at Mr.Doughnut, like a hit man in a great white coat,
his black eyes hot for me.
He'll take me to a long cave with labyrinthine corridors
grooved down to the hot-pap centre of the world.
There my belly will be sliced open, my innards sucked out
and devoured, my bones strewn on a desolate shore.
There is no doubt that I am on the verge of a
breakthrough.

I can feel substantial presences move over me.
I locate vesications of pain detailed in the smallest
object.
The parquet is so loud with individual voices I cannot
stand it.
I feel like a schizophrenic in a room of blood, my nerve
ends
shielded by the lightest membrane.
When passers-by knock on the frame doorway calling out my
name,
I cry bUckets.
I cry on provocation and everything provokes me.
O Deliverence swamp me!
Deliver me!
Nightly at two I move from the divan to a white futon
on the floor, in an airless empty bedroom.
Waiting.
Waiting.
Finally one night
Every sickness is made visual.

Heads fathoms wide
And as murky as Hudson soup
Fly at me,
Screaming,
Disembodied figures maul me,
Pulling at my skin
Until it stretches
Away from the bone,
Piling up in a gruesome heap
Of shredded meat.
A ravenous jet raven
Scoops up these pieces
Of my flesh,
Leaving one eye dangling
By a blue vein
From its beak.
Below I see my stock of bones
on a curve of golden sand,
My organs hanging
From the branches of a tree.

The room spins.
Bulbs push
From the patterned paper
on the wall.
Streams of green liquid
Tumble down.
Frogs come with it,
Tiny lugubrious women,
Diseased children,
Strutting vaginas
With mantillas,
Manacled penises
Holding bowls of tomato paste,
Teeth with TVs
In the cavities,
Templates of the holocaust.
Blades delivering
A kind of pain
No scream could fix.
My eyes relishing
The details.
Every violence
Ever imagined by me
Is perpetrated.
Shocking pink parents
Sew up their children's mouths.
Fathers feel their daughters.
Mothers eat their sons.
All things dark and blighted.
Fingers singed to sticks.
Water the colour of blood.
Death in the shape of quartz.

I stand merged in the secret current of all things.
Tones of the inanimate woven into the returned
structure of my body.
Refleshed in one way, resurrected in another.
The substance of this first death fluent in my blood.
The fever broken, my shadow reclaimed.
The break in my lifeline beginning to heal.
Here you can see for yourself.

29

LOVE OR BEDAMMED

It could have been
Northern Minnesota,
The lake frigid, black.
Surrounds of trees
Sworn plaintively in the soil.
We walked haphazardly
Along the mud track
In the aftermath of trucks
Lumbering cinnamon trunks
Of pine and sesquatian
Smells of resin
Fixed in the air
Like mixed aromas
Under a feminine hood.
Herons evoked the equatorial
Crashing into the canopy
Shaking limbs
Stretching into crested sinews
Becoming rigid in dominion.

On the timber bridge
She asked;
"Do you mind if I take your hand?"
Amazed that anyone would want to,
I said "No."
I was committed, loved.
I loved!
But surely this action
Did not work
Against the courtesy
Of my fidelity.
I hugged her, held her,
But did not rove my hand
Or let her bleed.
I felt a cinematic angle pan,
Zoom in.
Guilt
Sleezed its fingers between

This darkly enfolded couple.
The woman's head
Burrowed into his breast,
His head lofted,
Eyes open. Stiff.

At one with everything
She thought he felt the same.
The same would have given her more.
He had decided elsewhere
To abide
And would not be bidden
To fill the feminine
In a burly bed.
No pedestrian progenitor he,
No easy lay, no way
Was he willing to do anything
But comfort her in a strategy
Of arms and words.
No wriggly hero
Ready to rise
To her womanly size.
He said no
To this unknown woman
Lapsed on his breast,
But in the watery light
She glimpsed him blink
And like an egret
Vast over lazy minnows
Seized his lips.

HE BEGINS TO MOVE AWAY

He begins to move away
Before his last kiss
Has dusted my cheek.
He refuses to stand in the light
and his arm is like a coffin lid
Against my side.
No scream is loud enough
To alter this dereliction of me
Or unbind the complexity of his confusion.
He answers in a dead gutteral voice
Making me feel unworthy.
I do not reflect in his eyes
And his love of me is not
Holy or demanding.
When I cry he explains each tear
As defining the divisibility of my love.
He does not believe
that my tears are spun
From the centre of my love
For the image of my love.
He makes me cry
Because he does not touch me.
He says he loves me
But he moves away
To shine his words on brimstone,
To stare at his dried flowers,
To expound on the quality of his mercy
And the responsibility of his goodness.
I do not want him
To retreat past my last word.
Or see myself
According to his words
Beseeched in darkness.

NO TWO ARE THE SAME

No two are the same
Stones or treaties of love
Fingers or despoiled flowers
Songs of the rejoicing voice
Seeping into the current of time.
In this surrogate field
I stand by stones
Which match my life,
By roots that match my fingers,
Infusing blood,
Spelling in red-letter leaves
The legend of what is concentrated.

When I was young
I snapped the garters
Father had said would hold
The ribbed and knee-length cloth
Every young man needs
To preserve appearances
In this world.
When I was young
I could finalize no story
Or sweep past legions of eyes
Without falling to my knees
Or speak without dishevelling my anger.
When I was young
I rearranged my tongue
And learned the language of stones.

No two are the same
Dreams or memories
Versions of the past
Strung pearl by pearl
Hung on the chosen one
Who sings as you believe
You sing yourself,
Hung on the one who is waiting
To take the stone
Moistened on your tongue
And walk into the wilderness.

Frank Golden

When I was young
There were configured obstacles,
I ran without fear
Hurdling to the wildest corner,
A sanctuary on the island
Where no song was sung
That was not fully conjured
By words alone.
Now in this stone field
Altered by elemental graces
All things impart to me,
I walk with bare feet
On stones of individual memory,
Calling by its true name
All that is truly named.

FOR ALL THAT HAS GONE BEFORE

For all that has gone before,
Love threaded so darkly in the blood.
Hearts levered to the water.
Curses thickened on the strickened tongue.
Devils laid with garlic in the skin.

What sweetness there was
Is less memoried.
What bonds there were
Dissolved in our veins,
Leaving us an inheritance
Of deranging rites.

It seems an unrecorded
An unreachable light
That was loved.
What trust there was
Now magicked from memory
Leaving a legacy
Of non implorable hearts,
A jealousy of talents,
A dryness in our sour recourse
To language that seems only
To measure our hard time.

From under the burden
Of our distressed silence
No new information
Descended on us.
The dream downpour
That would have rinsed us
Tumbled on the less blighted.

On defensive days
Anger clamped us.
Rigid hypnotics
Delving and delivering
Selected words,
Whirring blades

Whittling and diminishing
Our undecided love.

In the yellow street
a constant taxi
Mourned our startling blood.
We waited for the inspired song
Visible in others
As an habitual light
To transform our cloned image
And cancel our frantic hands
Debauching in temper.

PART II

What is the use of making all these conjectures, of setting up imaginary premises?
Hamsun

For Frank — "En route to Bamenda" — '90
RELEASED IN THE IMAGE

BESIDE HIMSELF

In the Monaghan Sanatorium sunroom
He sucks his plush fingers
As though they were hawthorn buds
He had to polish with his spittle
For flowers to sprout.
Flowers for his mother, his wife,
His dead marriage.
Flowers for his bedside jamjar,
Eyes on the flowerless sweep of ground
Down to the river, tracks of mud
Churned with remnants of solar birds,
Cows' eyes, pitted tongues
Pink as honeycomb stones,
Inlaid with blue peas and sour rice,
While movements of kitchen swill
Curdle and brace the black river.

There are feet depressions
Beyond the french windows,
Cornflake pollen crushed for the man
Who rumps his butt like a beebee,
Cardboard rolls for new age crowns.
Goya's Kings and Bishops are here,
Elevated men of the mind
Wretching ornate proclamation.
An unreferenced aristocracy
Romping and enacting their just lives,
Missionary ghouls lording it with
Toothbrush croziers and Hail Worthy cocks,
Seeds rooted in their gums,
Seaweeds feeding on ear wax,
Gull droppings speckling their teeth,
Butterweeds rising from manure pits
between their thighs.
At ten they wait like pitch-stilled herons
For the rail sound of steel on marble,
The stacked tablet trolley laden
With ideal versions of themselves.
Treats to cauterize the roaming wound
And leave them warm in their unmemoried past,

39

Frank Golden

Where swells of the bloodiest anger
Are as remote as the rarest flower.

Blinds are drawn and neat shadows
Split their oblique heads.
Liquid white marble flows underneath
their chairs,
So clean, so pure,
And from the walls flow sloes,
Clusters of green nuts,
Sudden rashes of hot poker berries,
Tree limbs bathing in the milk-white river,
Fruits harmonizing the world.

A torpor mulls the head
And for a while makes abstract
The hard negotiation between flesh and blood.
When the brain blasphemes
Images he thought anaesthetized,
Move out from grave oblongs and decry
His hand in all things.
Dumpling women stand in the midnight light
With pilious wings and crimson eyeballs,
Pulling their vulvas wide
While the protean dead still rampant in his seed
Fall irretrievably from him,
Leaving his sac dry, his mind unprotected.
Leaving him mad as the day he flowered
over Monaghan town,
Kinked in the vision of a two-way mirror,
Bonded to his own blood,
Streaming into the centre of his bones.

ROSE GARDEN ADDENDUM

A halo of roses garland the union.
"Whisper the seed into my ear love."
"O my Darling
Cirsium Eriophorum.
This is our suffering profile.
We will never be equal again
Or love more severely.
You, I, will change,
We will become a family."

Now that everything has grown so quiet
We will celebrate in silence.
Shimmering trees hang over us
Our feet slide into the river,
Sun dapples our skin.
This is a commonplace bliss,
Thorns are elsewhere, but where?

In this perfumed zone
With milk legs and hawkweed crevices
One hysterical seed
Swims from the germing pool
And a dark baby colours our lives.
Will he make me sit in a different way?
Will he taint me with a functionless odour?
In the aftermath of being well pleased
Will he cause me to dream
Of God, Mullingar and sex?

Here is the simplest of roses my darling,
Its perfume the antidote
to your prospective suffering.
I will go to the highest hilltop
in Monaghan,
With rooks and ravens pecking
At the lovestore in my stomach,
And in a corrugated belvedere
Water my unremontant heart.

41

Frank Golden

Through a parting of willow limbs
I can see the extinction of our love.
When the child sings at your breast
I feel like a rich burgher
With no access to his mystic maid.
Gone is the crest line of rose stems
cut for you,
And in the gold field are standing flowers,
Signposts to a new order.

I too want to suck the breast fruit,
Plunge your nipples through my palms,
Rivet my body with your milk,
Understand the nature of what has been lost;
Your damp pleasure and attentive teeth,
Your loneliness for me,
Your feet at the centre of my life.
Now it is your son,
That extinguishing star, that dwindling whisper,
That happenstance saved in the belly,
Who shines in the light of your relaxed
wantonness,
While I maddened by what I cannot have
Sit hunched and brooding
Fallen from wonder,
Bowed in the rose garden.

COLDER THAN DEATH

My loneliness is greater
With you than without you.
Ancient sicknesses
Contrived together
Clot in the gullet.
On this starless night
When the words leave my head
Love will be a diminished thing
Between us. Dried billweed
Will litter your breast
And griege moss
Grow over your navel.
My dry tongue will shrivel
In your bush.
I will lapse by your side
Colder than death.

TERMINAL

Nothing is forgiven or forgotten.
Manias, obsessions, vengeances,
Curl from breakages in the skin.
Bowel worms laze on tufts of hair,
Crawl to the flexed neck cords
Up to the frozen head,
Where layers of the sallowest skin
Have been flayed off.
Eyes reflect a tension
Of barely contained innards.
The whole body looks reduced
As though contained by the lightest
Of membranes, a stomach sac
With carcinated entrails.

I see you as you were on Crow Street,
Back against the wall of a burned out
Pyjama factory, a mustachioed Pancho Villa
Stilled before the squad. Your nostrils
Barrel holes held up and flared
To pocket the flight of bullets
And snot them back in a return volley.
All of your life's hectic instants
Rubberized to fill the swollen third temple
In the centre of your forehead.
Memory digesting the bullet visited into your
skull,
An infection in your visionary horoscope.
Denied the expansion of your head
Earth now layers your flaggellated corpse.

DEAD SHEEP ON THE HILL

There are knives
In the white backs
Of just men
In a just war.
It is war,
Even though the sheep
Eat as before.
In the green ghetto
Love bullies the stranger.
Young girls offer themselves,
Telling him it is his right
As Conqueror
To take what he wants.
Take me.
They vie amongst themselves.
There are bullets
In the calves and buttocks
Of young women.
But it is not war.
The war is over.
Trees fruit,
The sun shines,
There are beautiful rotations
To be contemplated.
Only those who deny
There is no war
Feel the brunt of his justice.
And there is no war.
There are merely rhythms
of violence,
As there are rhythms
of love,
And green girls
Lay down before him
In the rough field.
They love him
He is the peacemaker.
His truth is,
There is no war
There is only justice.

Frank Golden

ILLUSTRIOUS CORPSES

Illustrious corpses is a thriller dealing with an investigation of murder which leads to a series of assassinations. A compelling study of political corruption.

DEATH BY HANGING

A young Korean fails to die during his hanging and cannot be hanged again until he acknowledges his guilt. Using Brechtian techniques the officials frantically try to persuade him of his guilt but it is only when they discover that he is innocent that he allows himself to be hanged. Thus challenging the right of the judges to judge him.

In Dublin Film Guide

A HOME FOR ITSELF

Rigid in the stone hive
A figure cleaves through salt water.
An enamelled mammoth tooth
With the symmetry of old blood fallen aside.
Her streaming hair moist as corntails,
Her amber eye pips divined by beetles,
Her fingers cool as limestone picks
On Shawe-Taylors marble altar.

The view past death is wet, mist laden.
The colour of death through this lancet window
Is green. A sap shade for emerald spiders,
Diminutive aggressors flowing over the dead.
Mixing blood, dust and light,
A dressing for snake wood in the vaulted den,
Where the tart body is hung out and left to dry.

On lichen ridges
Seven versions of the lover
Fold into mist.
From a tank of marsh grass
A man no bigger than a bull terrier
Lifts himself over the images
Of his dead lover.

Naked in the copper-green light
He gnaws on nightshade root
And sharpens the edge of his horror.
"In the flesh pots of Chang Mai
You sucked in their lair.
You were wanton from your soggy
Armpits to your cunt.
Buttterflies never rested on you."

His eyes roll. His head
Throwing up remembered colloquies;
Violences, brutalities, obscenities.
Wind singing the invidious nightmare
of their past.

47

Frank Golden

Man and woman dressed in disastrous moods,
Hatred as severe as steel,
Blood on their teeth and on their fingers.
Blood always on their minds.
Always a corporeal fetish.
Death lounging in their heads,
Tensing their fingers
When they handled knives.
Death always the great factor between them.
Death making a home for itself.

THE WORD ACCORDING TO GOD

In igneous light my sinews
Are attached to wood whorls.
Sisters pin the frame
Of earth wings to my arms.
"Lift away" they cry,
"To the great reference
Of your Father.
There!
Lift through that light chink
In the sky.
Wing it body and soul.
Fly with blood tapers streaming,
Angels singing,
Coral clouds thundering
A great oratorio."

"But Sisters, my longevity
Is in ancient heads.
My muscles are exhausted,
My blood as water.
I cannot leave you
With my meaning stranded.
Look!
Here is my body.
That is all that it is."

A JUST AND HOLY KILL

Seeds of the pomegranate,
Crimson pearls tucked into
The gill wound of his side.
On this Holy day,
Flesh falls in strips of foil
Into the kindled fire.
Copper conducters
Wire the vagina
Making it spill its cock.

Witness this freed man's head
Full of milk and densities of egg.
Hefted from the cross
Steadied by alder beams
Stitched into the elders hands,
He is taken to a vault
Where accreting teeth
Fall from the limescale roof.
Howls of rash dogs
Curdle pools of spilt blood.
Blood clotted in lobes
Thick as breasts,
Tears for the Almighty dead
Collected on a grooved platter,
A circular soak
Moving towards the first cause.

Christ pay no heed.
The very dead are stretchered
And decomposed, with black lungs
Full of rancid growths
And sexless tongues
Loose between their teeth.
Here blood is the image of truth
And hardens the ground
For circles of down.

Man and woman in this divinity
Both bulge about the cross shaft,

Hands in a heavenly synthesis
Conduct the spirit
Through to eternity,
Blue and white rags
Billow like seaweed tapers,
Crepe tails flowing
The soul's flamboyant release.

There is no wilder synaesthesia;
Cocked on the cross,
His sweet flesh covered
By tandem necrophiliacs,
Disclosing the geometry
Of the inverted,
While the flowing soul
Clasps the sacred rungs
Of Jacob's ladder upturned.
Its spaces spelling the legend,
This is a just and holy kill.

Frank Golden

IT'S VERY SIMPLE

It's very simple: what are we gaining - excuse me if I'm repeating
myself - what are we gaining by a pragmatism that robs our life
of poetry, dreams, mysticism - are these all lies? What is truth?
Can you tell me that? We can only struggle along by using
symbols and we change them as we alter our views. By the way,
let's not neglect our drinks.
Hamsun

A dream sings in my head and flies me to the four corners
Where bleak waters tremble and reptiles taste the marrow
of curved horns.
Worms and whispers breed in the skin
Roving out through pores dripping with foxgloves.
Enshrouded women redden in a monsoon dust storm.
Blood trickles from the tile roof into the water bucket.
My family are all dead and a raven and white bear
foreshadow my life.
I search for the ju ju tree and walk along the Rine,
Looking for ten round stones to describe a Phythagorean
divinity.
No one sees me do anything at all,
I am elsewhere in the wilderness.

PART 3

What you need now is peace and quiet
Kundera

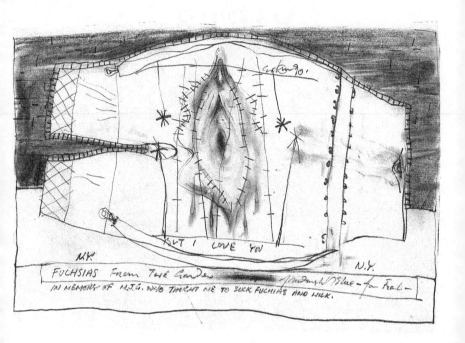

ELIZA ELIZA

I have ground red cherries to a paste like the warm men
of the South Pacific,
Clumping it on a pearl hook waiting for the sappy vulva
of my love to snap like an elusive apple fish.
O Eliza Eliza don't run to the sweet potato garden,
Run to the nut grove where tubes of semen hang
by phallocryptic gourds.
Let me put oyster urine in your bethel pouch
And avocado stones in a circle round your bed.
Tell me Eliza that you'll listen to the love pleas
of a north Clare farmer,
Just down in Lisdoonvarna for the day.

O Eliza Eliza I'm no Spanish hidalgo with bull's blood
breeding maggots underneath my fingernails.
I don't sing from eucalyptus trees or tie musk leaves
around my balls.
I'm a north Clare farmer with goat kids on the hill
and a good quota and fair land.
I sit on round stones in the long field when the
weather's cool,
And think of succulent women soft and rich as wild
mangoes.

O Eliza I bet your breasts are white as coconuts
and your nipples hot as chilli peppers and as long,
And don't worry now Eliza 'bout your pimples,
I'm not a man like Ruskin about to faint at the sight
of a blackhead or two.
Sure we'll rove the body like mine sweepers freeing
the least hummock of its pus,
And talk on winter nights with the bed pulled up close
to the fire,
Of taboos and sago fields and how the girls in Tonga
sit on plump cushions to keep their buttocks soft,
And how the chief's daughter is oiled each evening
in the rosegrey light,
And how in the lime Marquesian islands there is a ritual
display of the young girls with their legs asunder.

O Eliza Eliza chomp on my lips as though they were
tender spinach stalks.
Sink in with me against the turmoil of these blustery
north Clare winds.
Let me scent you with fennel, parsley and sage.
Let me nuzzle the milk mound of your navel.
Let me love you to the curlews dipping cry.
O Eliza Eliza can't you hear the cowrie shells
in the taro garden echo your name,
And the cormorants off Black Head telling you
I'm a good man.
A man finally fit for sanctuary.
O Eliza Eliza come to me.

SING SING O MY MOST CHASTENED HEART

My tongue on the new road from Gort
Was stiff as a rabbit's tail after a full moon.
I lost everything walking towards Mars,
Yellow as Billy Vaughan's jaundiced son.
My legs temporarily rooted to the spot
Where my career prospects as a lover
Were rigidly demeaned.

When I think of our love
I think there were more Hallelujas
In a jar of swimming wasps.

When I think of our love
I think of blue Madonna frogs
Raking worms with their forefeet.

When I think of our love
I think of wolf spiders
Rapacious after a good hump.

O but there's nothing I'd like better
Than to have you back in the clamp,
Watch you reek over my meter
And ordinance a different man.
You know you had in your rhythm
In your state-of-the-art tongue,
Your horsey buttocks
Thumping me into the duvet.

O I want you back
To twirl the curl of hair
Around my bellybutton,
And feast with your discoloured teeth
On my pristine flesh.
I want your sloot valve to sauce me,
Your hands to slub me
Your teeth to spile me
Your lips to scoff me
Our lives to merge
This love to pound on longer.

Frank Golden

BRIEVARY FOR A SUMMER NIGHT

You fell from stone into a dark grave of night-blue
heather,
With showers of meteorites singing in silver,
Making everyone's prospect seem greater,
Making us feel less diminished.
The two of us falling after memory,
Kneeling in sight of Kilmacduagh,
The great tower rising as a confluence of energies,
Leading us remotely to the bridge by Poulataggle
With high water fluent as an amniotic surround,
Its whispering code gurgled into poontang breaches.

Perhaps we have left too much underground,
In bowls of earth and caves where ancient bears
shivered and died;
Left too much unuttered,
Histories clotted in the wrist,
Freed in the dream of marching soldiers
And malignant spectres flowing in the angle
of the room.
Odd shapes leaving a ghostly odour,
Leaving us to circulate in thin air.

We hold out calmly for the transfer of blood,
Knowing perhaps that we find our greatest excitement
apart.
Denying this we step inside the derelict caravan,
Decorated with relics of the sixties.
We push self-portraits, saris, boxes of paints
and posters to one side,
Leaving the bed tossed with blankets and exotic rugs,
a shanty lamp glowing crimson,
Our feet colder than chancel limestone,
Our hearts enduringly secret.
The clinging heat melting the little language left to us,
Letting our bodies grieve to a temporary succinctness.

THE MEN OF CLARE NOW DRINK THEIR PORTER ON THE PALISADES

With the yellow flesh of mussels from Poulnaclogga
still rotting in their cavities,
They board the number one on Broadway for Inwood
and the Bronx.
Big boys with their mothers' eyes in their eyes.
Limestone eaters, cave dwellers, with heron feathers
stitched like scapulars into their buttocks,
And Toonarossa holly sprouting from clay packs
between their toes,
And salt water from Dunbalcaun Bay passing for urine
through their bladders.
On windless days they scale Chanin, Chrysler and
Rockefeller,
Overview this canyon terrain with chemical stacks
on New Jersey wasteland,
And gangland shells blistering the south Bronx.
Visions of ridges and defiles among the pencil avenues
scoring the city,
Recalling silver outcrops past Loch Aleenaun,
And stone escarpments on the crest of Black Head.
It leaves their heads thinly present, memories pecking
the cranial shell
On the subway list and rock to Marble Hill,
Where they buy six packs of Guinness,
Head down Independence Avenue to the Conrail line,
and from their perch on Devils Rock,
Spit their ferocious yearning into the waters of
Spuyten Duyvil.

59

Frank Golden

BUTTOCK TO BUTTOCK

You were my buttermilk bride
Taken on the hay rick
In the rich Western climate.
Sun brilliant on the turquoise belts
past Capanawalla,
On the stiff road to Fanore beach.
My stone hand on your wired bra,
Listening to the sucking fuschias
Plural in the grid crust of the Burren,
These were our egg Sundays
And raspberry seed afternoons,
Fandangoes stepped in the bullion of ragwort,
Nudes collapsed over mushroom stones,
Our ligger fingers denting flesh
perfected like cream,
Drawing dragon flies to our tits
Until we were dressed with aboriginal flair,
Blue-pronged wings like emu tracks
Circulating to our abdomens.
Bush folk in search of the bush soul
Clicking in the seed grass,
Equatorial and dense over our heads.
My head at your centre,
Feasting at the loose entrance,
Bells ringing, the zoned spirit
Released in the image of a boat,
Moodily drawn onto fathomless rings.
The scent of our fever sugaring the air,
Making us look like breakwater angels
Or lubberly children teething into each others
Gums, linking whatever could be linked,
Squeezing out an hilarious country energy,
Snoozing to our first post,
With stems of burnet in our crisp teeth,
The wired bra bent out of shape forever.
Our slouch bodies buttock to buttock
Buttermilk groom and Bog bride.

THE YOUNGEST OF MY MOST MOURNFUL LOVERS

My greatest premonitions have steadied me in advance
for heartfelt and weighty tribulations.
One deranged day in September,
With clouds fertile on the shoulder of Cathair Mhor,
I saw the youngest of my most mournful lovers
scratch a black note,
Claiming her Virgo decision must be made against me.
A prophecy of moons and tides,
A vision of life's course going against her
If she stayed to shamanize and run the coral of her
heart over my face,
If she cried into her wilderness and came out
with shielas dripping from her teeth,
If she stayed and whispered violations into my ear,
If she ran on islands of moonlight
Flowing her hands over moonraked devils,
If she coupled again in starred hayfields sweating milk,
If she heard the echo of her love return a thousand times
shattering the harmony of her image.

The virility of new love lightens the whole world,
It picks three words from the lexicon and memorizes
eternity.
The blackest night is a richness of subtleties,
The natural world utterly spun in their blood,
No heart stands aside from them.
They tenderize the howls of dogs
And are thick and impermeable,
Full of the flesh of love.
They stand on Burren limestone in the glistening mizzle,
Walking through fields of barley to the shattered
windmill
Overlooking Kinvara and the districts of Moy and
Capacushie,
Laying down under tassel-braids of barley,
Rain spilling on their heads and in their eyes,
Storm-lovers fast against the sharpest turn of wind.

O I saw the youngest of my most mournful lovers

scratch a black note,
Claiming her Virgo decision must be made against me.
A prophecy of moons and tides,
A vision of life's course going against her
If she stayed to shamanize and run the coral of her
heart over my face.

MAURA RUA

When the light of this crinniu moon mulls over
the battlements of Leameneh castle,
Allow me to kneel under your magnificent thighs Maura Rua
And with razor teeth clip the thick hairs on your shins,
Food rich enough to fill my belly for a year.
Allow no more English fornicators to lap your nipple milk
Or smooch their swill tongues on your meaty lobes.

We'll foray again like you did with Conor O'Brien
in the forties,
And relieve invested settlers like Gregory Hickman
of Barntick,
Of everything they own, hogs, griddles, sheep, bales of
wool
Sides of beef, running fowl, geese and all their lands.
We'll ride the spirit trails of North Clare,
From the great cairn at Poulawack through Gleninsheen and
onto Cathair Mhor,
Turning our horseshoes backwards to confuse the enemy.

I want to love you Maura Rua, daughter of Turlough Roe
Mac Mahon late of Clonderalaw.
I want to come to you in the great regal room at Leameneh
Where your host of ravens perch above you in a circle.
I want to plunge my hands under samite silk and crepe
petticoats bell-sweeping from your waist,
And hold your opulent body naked but for the pendant
dolphin swimming in your breast inlet.
I want to reek of your succulence and not relent until
you have managed yourself over my love.

I tell you now I understand your just hatreds.
When Ludlow and his men killed Conor at Inchicronin
in fifty one,
You did what you had to, to preserve your lands intact.
Majestic tactician that you were you took Cooper
the Cromwellian to your bed,
Bore him a menial species and when a safe time had
elapsed,

63

Kicked his encumbering body from the battlements.

O let me kneel Maura Rua under your magnificent thighs
And milk your spirit like the miraculous cow Glas Gaibhne
for the good of your people.
By the heat of the great fire let me uncurl rich ferns
from the bowls of your armpits,
And feed on luscious winged insects ancestral in your
blood.
Let me organize my tongue in the geometry of your
solacing wound,
And love the russet body of a Clare woman who did not
cower or tremble,
When those Cromwellian butchers Stace and Apers,
Destroyed our Burren tribes and spent themselves
In the dead bodies of valiant women in the townlands
of Teeska and Kilinaboy.

You have flushed the bad seed of Cooper from your bowels
And laid to rest the baby he kindled in you.
Come with me Maura onto the battlements of Leameneh
castle,
Let me pressure forever the scope of my love,
Let us retain between us the rigid instincts of our people.